D1226471

Thomas Edison

A Buddy Book
by
Rebecca Gómez

ABDO
Publishing Company

VISIT US AT
www.abdopub.com

Published by Buddy Books, an imprint of ABDO Publishing Company, 4940 Viking Drive, Suite 622, Edina, Minnesota 55435. Copyright © 2003 by Abdo Consulting Group, Inc. International copyrights reserved in all countries. No part of this book may be reproduced in any form without written permission from the publisher.

Printed in the United States.

Edited by: Christy DeVillier
Contributing Editors: Matt Ray, Michael P. Goecke
Image Research: Deborah Coldiron
Graphic Design: Jane Halbert
Cover Photograph: Library of Congress
Interior Photographs: Getty Images, Henry Ford Museum, North Wind Picture Archives

Library of Congress Cataloging-in-Publication Data

Gómez, Rebecca.
    Thomas Edison / Rebecca Gómez.
        p. cm. — (First biographies. Set III)
    Includes index.
    Summary: An introduction to the life of the man who developed the electric light bulb and many other inventions.
    ISBN 1-57765-945-7
    1. Edison, Thomas A. (Thomas Alva), 1847-1931—Juvenile literature. 2. Inventors—United States—Biography—Juvenile literature. [1. Edison, Thomas A. (Thomas Alva), 1847-1931. 2. Inventors. 3. Scientists.] I. Title.

TK140.E3 G654 2003
621.3' 092—dc21
[B]
                                                          2002074672

Table Of Contents

Who Is Thomas Edison?

Thomas Edison was a great inventor. Thanks to Edison, people enjoy recorded music, movies, and electric lights.

Edison is famous for bringing electric light to people's homes. Before Edison, people used candles, gas lamps, and oil lamps. But these lights were unsafe. Edison gave people a safe way to light up their streets and homes.

Thomas Edison

Growing Up

Thomas Alva Edison was born on February 11, 1847. He was born in Milan, Ohio.

Thomas's family moved to Port Huron, Michigan, when he was seven years old. Young Thomas was a very curious boy. But he did not do well in school. So, Thomas's mother taught him at home.

Thomas Edison as a young man.

Thomas loved to read. He enjoyed learning about science. He began doing experiments at home.

At age 12, Thomas got a job. He worked for the Grand Trunk Railway. Thomas rode on the train and sold newspapers to travelers. His train traveled from Port Huron to Detroit. Thomas did experiments during the long train ride.

Young Edison grew up to invent this electric train.

A Young Hero

One day at work, Edison saw a boy in danger. The boy was on the train tracks. A train was coming toward the boy. Edison scooped up the boy and saved his life.

The boy's father worked for the train station. He thanked Edison and taught him an important skill. He taught young Edison how to use a telegraph machine.

Thomas Edison and a telegraph machine.

Telegraph Expert

Before telephones, people used telegraphs to send messages. Thomas Edison got a job as a telegrapher in 1863. He became an expert telegrapher. But he got in trouble for doing experiments at work.

Edison changed jobs many times. At age 20, he moved to Boston. He began working for Western Union. This was a big telegraph company.

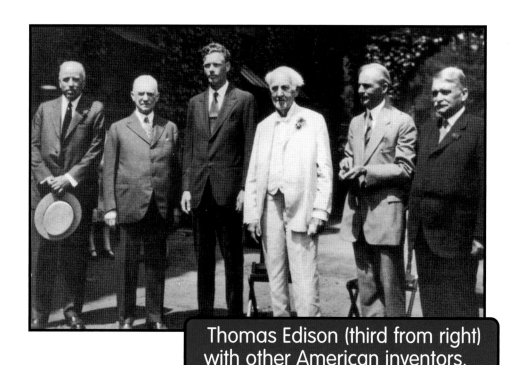

Thomas Edison (third from right) with other American inventors.

In Boston, Edison met other inventors. He set up a workshop with them. Edison quit his job so he could be an inventor. He made many inventions. One was an electric vote counter.

Young Inventor

In 1869, Thomas Edison moved to New York City. He was very poor. But he did not give up making inventions.

One day, Edison invented a stock ticker. A company bought it for $40,000. Edison used this money to work on more inventions.

Edison had many useful inventions.

Thomas Edison (right) with another famous inventor, Henry Ford.

Edison married Mary Stillwell in 1871. In 1876, the Edison family moved to Menlo Park, New Jersey. Edison built his own workshop there. He called it an "invention factory." He hired talented people to work with him.

Edison's Lightbulb

Before 1877, there was no machine for recording sounds. People could not listen to recorded music. Thomas Edison invented a machine that recorded and played back sounds. It was called the phonograph.

Thomas Edison and his phonograph.

Edison and his team worked hard to invent a working lightbulb.

After the phonograph, Edison began working on a new invention. He tried inventing an electric lightbulb that was safe and cheap. Edison and his team worked for more than a year. They tested hundreds of lightbulbs.

In 1879, Edison tested a lightbulb that burned for about 40 hours. This was Edison's first big success with electric light. Right away, he made plans to make his lightbulb better.

People began calling Edison the "Wizard of Menlo Park."

Edison wanted people to enjoy electric lights in their homes. In 1882, Edison set up the world's first power station. This station brought electricity to many homes in New York City.

More Inventions

Edison's wife died in 1884. Two years later, he married Mina Miller. They had three children.

In 1887, Edison opened a new workshop in West Orange, New Jersey. It was much bigger than his Menlo Park workshop. At one time, about 10,000 people worked there.

Thomas Edison's workshop at Menlo Park.

Edison invented many other useful things. He invented a new phonograph that played wax records. He also invented a moving-picture camera.

Edison made the first movies with his moving-picture camera.

Edison Facts

- Thomas Edison's first workshop was in the basement of his family's home. At that time, he was only 10 years old.

- Thomas Edison had serious hearing problems.

- Edison had 1,093 patents. A patent shows who owns the idea for an invention.

- A British inventor, Joseph Swan, invented a lightbulb before Thomas Edison.

- The first words recorded on Edison's phonograph were "Mary had a little lamb."

- In 1878, President Rutherford B. Hayes invited Edison to the White House. He showed the president his phonograph.

- The phonograph was Edison's favorite invention.

A Great Inventor

On October 18, 1931, Thomas Alva Edison died. He was 84 years old.

Thomas Edison had many ideas. Testing each idea was hard work. Edison failed many times. But he believed each failure taught him something. Thomas Edison did not give up easily. This may be why he was such a great inventor.

Thomas Edison's inventions changed the world.

Important Dates

February 11, 1847 Thomas Alva Edison is born in Milan, Ohio.

1859 Young Edison begins working for the Grand Trunk Railway.

1863 Edison becomes a telegraph operator.

1868 Edison invents an electric vote counter.

1876 Edison opens his own workshop in Menlo Park, New Jersey.

1877 Edison invents the phonograph.

1879 Edison invents an electric lightbulb that burns for 40 hours.

1882 The world's first power station opens.

1887 Edison's new workshop in West Orange, New Jersey, opens.

1891 Edison shows off his moving-picture camera.

October 18, 1931 Thomas Edison dies.

Important Words

electric describes something that uses electricity. Electricity powers many things like lights and televisions.

experiment a special test. People often learn something from an experiment.

invent to make something for the first time. People who invent are called inventors. They create inventions.

lightbulb the part of an electric lamp that gives off light.

phonograph a machine that plays recorded sounds.

stock ticker a machine that shows company stock prices.

telegraph a machine used to send messages across wires.

Web Sites

Edison National Historic Site
www.nps.gov/edis/home.htm
Early Edison recordings, early movies, a tour of Edison's home, and other "Edisonia" are featured here.

Edison Elementary School
www.minot.k12.nd.us/mps/edison/edison/edison.html
Learn more about Thomas Edison and take a quiz to test your knowledge.

Index